# TELL THE WORLD

## A JESUS PEOPLE MANUAL

### ARTHUR BLESSITT

BEHOLD, I STAND AT THE DOOR, AND KNOCK: IF ANY MAN HEAR MY VOICE, AND OPEN THE DOOR, I WILL COME IN TO HIM, AND WILL SUP WITH HIM, AND HE WITH ME.
REVELATION 3:20

BUT AS MANY AS RECEIVED HIM, TO THEM GAVE HE POWER TO BECOME THE SONS OF GOD, EVEN TO THEM THAT BELIEVE ON HIS NAME
JOHN 1:12

**Fleming H. Revell Company**
**Old Tappan, New Jersey**

Scripture quotations in this volume are from the *King James Version of the Bible*.

ISBN 0-8007-0487-8

Copyright © 1972 by Fleming H. Revell Company
All Rights Reserved
Library of Congress Catalog Card Number: 78-177397
Printed in the United States of America

# *Contents*

# TELL THE WORLD
## A JESUS PEOPLE MANUAL

# The Jesus Revolution Is On!

The gospel in bars, go-go clubs, massage parlors, homosexual nightclubs, pornographic bookstores. The gospel on the streets, sidewalks, beaches, and in business establishments. Blitzes on high schools, shopping centers, and entire cities. The revolution is here, and every Christian must be constantly seeking greater opportunities to spread the Word.

The idea of revolutionary Christians is certainly nothing new. The New Testament Christians were revolutionaries. Every time they went to town, the people called out the Roman national guard or the lion squad. The Christians—so small in number—terrified them because they were filled with the dynamic power of the Holy Spirit.

Paul probably caused more riots and arrests than any other person in his day. Even Jesus Himself was considered a rebel against the established order. He was condemned by the religious leaders because He associated with drunkards, prostitutes, and thieves. But when the scribes and Pharisees criticized Him for this He had an answer ready. "They that are well need not a physician, but they that are sick. For I am not come to call the righteous, but sinners, to repentence" (Mark 2:17).

Somehow, despite the compelling example of our Lord, modern-day Christians have become fearful of associating themselves with anything that might cause eyebrows to be lifted. Many of us are so concerned about our reputations that we're afraid to take part in anything if we think anyone might condemn our actions. The goal of winning the world is okay, we feel, just as long as we're not asked to risk anything—our reputation or our comfortable, secure way of life, for instance.

Like the rich young ruler who went away sorrowful when Jesus told him to sell what he had and give to the poor, many of us are hung up on the thought that an all-out stand for Jesus might deprive us of some of our possessions.

Now, contrast that attitude with Jesus' view. He ". . . made himself of no reputation," the Bible tells us, and "took upon him the form of a servant, . . . and became obedient unto death, even the death of the cross" (Philippians 2:7).

You remember His words, "For what shall it profit a man if he shall gain the whole world and lose his own soul?" (Mark 8:36). The person who has eternal life should no longer be defeated by temporal values. When He said, "And ye shall know the truth, and the truth shall make you free" (John 8:32), I believe He meant *really* free—free to be obedient to Him, free of intimidation, free to walk in His way with regard to nothing else.

The time in which we live is critical. The need is astounding, and the laborers are few. Therefore, we must devise our tactics carefully, heeding the advice of Jesus to be "wise as serpents and harmless as doves."

**This book is a manual that explains how to exercise our Christian freedom in witnessing to our faith and winning others for Christ. How to communicate, how to revolutionize your neighborhood, your city, and the whole world is the subject of this book. In it, you'll find ways to share your spiritual vision, commitment, and enthusiasms— dozens of ways to accomplish the purpose of Jesus Christ on earth in this generation.**

**The tactics I am sharing with you are ones I have used myself, and found effective in getting the gospel known. This book will tell you how to witness in bars, brothels, and pornographic bookstores, as well as on buses and airplanes and in schools, and in dozens of other places in an attempt to confront the world with the living message of Jesus Christ.**

## POINTERS FOR WITNESSING

● Be sure that you are saved—that you have personally invited Jesus into your heart and fully accepted Him as your Saviour and Lord.

● You need to be filled with the Holy Spirit. "Not by might, nor by power, but by my Spirit, sayeth the Lord of hosts" (Zechariah 4:6).

● Any time you go out to work for Jesus you need to have a complete belief that what you're going out to do will be accomplished. There's no point in making an attempt if you don't think anything will be achieved. Many people are defeated before they begin because they don't really think anything can happen. Well, you have to have more faith than that. You have to believe that when you go out you are an instrument in God's hands and He will determine the outcome.

● Have a pleasant attitude. Even if you're burdened deep in your heart, outwardly you must be pleasant. How can you hope to win anyone unless you look like you've got something that somebody else might want to have? I remember, when God called me to preach, I thought, Lord, I don't want to be some old, double-chinned, potbellied, miserable-faced preacher! I want to *live*. And then I read the words of Christ, "I am come that they might have life, and that they might have it more abundantly" (John 10:10). It's the *abundant* life that we're to live with Him, and your attitude should reflect it.

● Don't be negative. Always be *for* something and avoid arguing about side issues. Here's an example of what I mean. If I'm marching in front of a pornographic bookstore and someone asks, "Are you against this store?" I don't say yes; instead, I tell them, "Well, I'm for the best book, and that's the Bible, and when you have that book you don't need these dirty ones."

● Don't be antagonistic. Your objective is to attract and win people, not to repel them and turn them off. Controversy, arguing, debating—these tactics never work. If someone wants to start an argument, just say, "May we have a moment of prayer?" or smile and say, "Jesus loves you," and walk away. We don't need to defend Jesus, we need to share him.

● Always be nonviolent. Violence will only create violence, as hate produces hate and anger produces anger. Therefore, it's never advisable to show anger. The weakest weapons we have are violent ones. Choose instead the most powerful weapon at our disposal. That weapon is love. Remember that God is with you and has promised He'll never forsake you.

● Be careful to stay within the law, but at the same time don't be afraid of arrest. If your reputation is so precious to you that you're afraid to risk having it stained, your effectiveness will be seriously diminished.

● You must even be prepared to die, if it comes to that. We have to be as willing to jeopardize our lives for Christ as the police or soldiers are willing to jeopardize theirs in the line of duty. How much more important are the souls of men! I would say that the mission is not worth doing if it isn't worth our lives. For too long we have pointed our finger, sat in our pew, watched our TV—it's time to get out and go into the center of the trouble or need and minister there.

**What are we trying to do? Our goal is to launch a mighty revolution for Christ by leading lost individuals to Him. This means explaining to others how in the eyes of God each of us has sinned and come short of His glory, and how sin separates us from God. We must spread the word that Jesus died on the cross, rose again and lives today, and that we must put our trust in Him and invite Him to come into our hearts and cleanse us from our sin. We need to let it be known that when we give our life to God we receive salvation and are born into His kingdom. When He enters our hearts to stay, we become His children, and having received Him, we need to get involved in fellowship with other believers, to be baptized and grow in His way—in Bible study, in prayer, and in witnessing.**

## COMMUNICATION AIDS

In my ministry I use a great many communication aids. These include printed materials such as tracts, Jesus stickers, and Jesus papers as well as the very effective Jesus cheers, and of course the Bible, all of which are described below. All can be a big help in getting through to people we need to reach.

● **Tracts** are small pieces of paper containing gospel messages, usually instructions on how a person may receive Jesus as his Saviour and Lord. There may be a prayer inviting Jesus into the individual's life, and instructions on what to do after he is saved. Tracts are very inexpensive, and they are tremendously effective in presenting the message of Jesus Christ.

● **Jesus stickers** are small circular pieces of adhesive paper carrying messages such as: JESUS LOVES YOU, TURN ON TO JESUS, and SMILE—GOD LOVES YOU. We started using Jesus stickers years ago. As a matter of fact, we introduced them. Ours are on red day-glo, about the size of a half-dollar, with the peace symbol on the bottom and a cross on top. They say: THE WAY TO HAVE PEACE IS THROUGH JESUS CHRIST. THERE'S REAL PEACE AT THE FOOT

OF THE CROSS. Because of their color, we call them reds. In the drug scene, drugs called downers are known as reds, and sometimes we'll go up to somebody and say, "Hey, man, can I turn you on to some reds?" Then we hit him with a little red Jesus sticker. It's a good way to start a conversation and to reach kids with the message of Christ.

● **Jesus papers** are Christian underground newspapers. Hundreds are being printed by different groups all over the country. They tell what's happening for Jesus in their particular city and deliver gospel messages in a kind of hip underground subculture direction.

● **Jesus Cheers.** In marches, shopping center meetings, beach rallies, and many other activities, Jesus cheers have been a very significant part of my own personal ministry. Sometimes people ask why you would do a cheer. They feel that it's out of place to cheer for Jesus.

But I take issue with that. At baseball games we cheer over a guy trying to hit a ball with a stick. At football games we cheer at getting an oblong ball over a line. At bowling alleys we cheer because a ball knocked down a bunch of pins. In fact, at all kinds of ball games people get excited and cheer. We cheer for politicians. We cheer for just about everything imaginable, so why is it that when we begin to express our faith in Jesus Christ in this way somebody is likely to think we're nuts?

On the contrary, we *should* express this joy. It is Scriptural to let our enthusiasm show for Jesus. The early Christians shouted and sang and cheered the victories that God won in their own lives and in their nation. I think it is the most appropriate thing in the world for Christians to cheer. One day someone asked me why I shouted. I said, "I'm practicing for heaven!"

Jesus cheers can be done just about any place. For instance, you can do a Jesus cheer during a lull at a basketball game in the gym. All you have to do is get about twenty-five kids together, and when there's a quiet time in the game somebody can stand up and lead a Jesus cheer. You can witness to thousands and thousands of people during basketball games, and you can do the same thing at baseball games and football games.

You can do Jesus cheers at a hamburger stand. You can witness to everyone within hearing by doing Jesus cheers at drive-in restaurants or down at the beach. Or if you have a carload of six or eight kids driving down a street you can roll all the windows down and do Jesus cheers. Even if you're just walking down the street, a group of ten, fifteen, or twenty kids can go along doing Jesus cheers and singing. Sometimes you can even cheer in church. Here are some of the Jesus cheers we do:

Give me a *J* (*Response:* **J**)
Give me an *E* (**E**)
Give me an *S* (**S**)
Give me a *U* (**U**)
Give me an *S* (**S**)
What does that spell? (**JESUS**)
What will get you higher than acid? (**JESUS**)
What will keep you up longer than speed (**JESUS**)
What will make you feel better than booze, or chicks, or any-
  thing else in the whole wide world? (**JESUS**)
What does America need? (**JESUS**)
What does the whole world need? (**JESUS**)
What are you going to do with him? (**GO, GO, GO**)

**RAH RAH RUE—JESUS LOVES YOU.**
**RAH RAH RE—JESUS LOVES ME**

**ONE WAY, JESUS WAY.**
**ONE WAY, JESUS WAY.**

How good is Jesus? (*Response:* **YUM YUM**)

You can make up your own cheers, and you can change those cheers any way you want. For instance, if you're in Los Angeles your cheer might be, What does LA need? And of course the answer comes back, **JESUS.** In New York you can use the same cheer, simply by changing the name of the city.

● **The Bible.** I always carry a Bible with me when I wit-ness. I read the Bible and show the person I'm talking to the passage of Scripture I'm reading. I'm not ashamed to carry the Word. People reach into their pockets to pull out a pack of cig-arettes and light up without shame. We should not fear to reach

The King's Library

into our pocket, pull out the Bible, and light up on the eternal light.

You have now learned how to prepare yourself for the great opportunity of witnessing and what you should try to accomplish. Where and how can you put this knowledge to work? The opportunities are endless. A wide variety are described in detail in this book.

# *Opportunities to Witness*

---

## STORES SELLING PORNOGRAPHIC LITERATURE

The part of California where I live has been called the smut and pornography capital of the world. Books and films depicting in detail every imaginable form of perverted sex are readily available to anyone who wants to buy them. There is big money in this business, which has helped organized crime to get a firm foothold in the area.

It is a dirty business from beginning to end. Even getting models—usually attractive-looking young girls—to pose is often done in an underhanded, not to say illegal, way. An agent will find a young girl on the street and comment on her good looks, asking her if she would like to be a model. Flattered, and often broke, she is almost sure to be interested. He promises her a sizable fee (which he has no intention of paying) and takes her to the studio. When she begins to realize what she is supposed to do, she is likely to refuse, however this doesn't faze the photographers. They've handled such problems many times before. After taking a few conventional shots of the girl with her clothes on, someone brings her a glass of water, to which a drug has been added to make her more cooperative. When the drug has taken effect, she is willing to pose any way she is asked to.

Here is a way you can fight the people who sell the filthy printed materials that result from this kind of operation:

Locate all of the pornographic bookstores in your area. Get a good supply of tracts, Jesus stickers, etc. Have two or three individuals enter the store, just like other customers, only instead of reading the dirty books, insert gospel tracts in as many as possible. In other words, just walk along and flip open a book and stuff a tract inside. In this manner you can blitz the store. If you're caught all they can do is throw you out; they don't know how many tracts you've already put in or at what page. When some backslider buys a dirty book and opens it up in his room, there's the Word of God on page seventy-eight! It just blows his whole trip.

Another attack that I've used successfully is to go to a pornographic bookstore and ask the manager if he will give me a rack to offer free Bibles. I've found that some of these stores will let you do this if you'll furnish the Bibles and keep the rack stocked. You stamp the Bibles inside "Not to Be Sold," and have one little area there, maybe right by the cash register, where they're on display. This is an effective way of witnessing in pornographic bookstores.

If you're making an attack in an attempt to close the store, you need to organize a group of really committed Christians who will begin with you and not stop until what you set out to accomplish has been completed. For this approach, you load up with tracts, Jesus stickers, and posters that you have made. Then you post some pickets outside the store. (Be sure they keep marching, so they won't be arrested for loitering or blocking the sidewalk.)

It's good to use girls as pickets, along with some guys. Girls are very effective, carrying signs saying: SEX IS MORE THAN A FIVE-DOLLAR LOOK, or WOULD YOU WANT YOUR DAUGHTER POSING FOR A DIRTY BOOK? or WOULD YOU LIKE YOUR SON IN A HOMOSEXUAL MAGAZINE?

Station at least one witness at either side of the entrance, making sure they stand at least ten feet from the door so they can't be arrested for blocking the entrance. These people will pass out tracts, Jesus papers, Bibles, and stickers, talking to the customers as they enter or leave and sharing Christ with them. A real shocker is for someone to stand outside and say to someone about to go in, "Hey, friend, I've got a book here that is so hot they've even banned it in there." He'll freak out to discover that it's the Bible!

Your pickets need to keep marching out front and your witnesses need to keep witnessing for as long as the store is open. This is almost a guaranteed way of closing it down. You see, many of the people buying books are supposedly Christians, and they have a guilty conscience. The picketing and witnessing do two things—they thin out the number of customers coming in, and they also call the attention of the entire community to the problem.

## PORNOGRAPHIC BOOKS AND MAGAZINES

Pornographic books and magazines may be found wherever all kinds of magazines and paperback books are displayed—in drugstores, liquor stores, and supermarkets. There are several ways this problem can be attacked. Many times you can just place a supply of small gospels in the racks with the other materials; just kind of move something back and place a stack of Gospels of John there instead. Or you may ask the manager if you can either have a section in one of the stands where you can put Bibles, or put up a display of free gospel material beside the magazine rack or newspaper stand.

Another way is, every time you are in one of these places, insert tracts in some of the books. If you're buying a newspaper, slip a tract in the paper below it. There are good opportunities to witness by placing material in and around magazine racks, especially those that are displaying pornographic books.

## NIGHTCLUBS

In planning a nightclub strategy, you have to decide whether you'll just make an overnight stop, a one or two or three-day blitz, or continue to keep entering the establishment and begin an outreach ministry. Or maybe your goal will be to close the place down. If you want to be able to go into the club and witness, don't start demonstrating against it, because once you put pickets up outside you probably won't be allowed to continue going in anymore. You'll lose your chance to talk to the people inside. So you have to decide which approach to take in each case. Sometimes I've done it one way and sometimes another. You must choose which course you'll take, according to how you feel led by the Lord at that particular time.

If you want to have a nightclub rally, go to a place where they have entertainment and ask to speak to the owner. Many times I've done this and just told him I wanted to have a Jesus rally inside the nightclub. This has been a very effective way to get the chance to speak. A lot of times the owner has agreed to give me ten minutes when I could get up between bands and bring some kind of evening devotion. After I preach and give the invitation for people to commit their lives to Christ, I tell them I'll meet them over on the side at the end of the service so they can come up and talk with me.

If you decide to start a night-life ministry in a nightclub, again begin by going right to the owner himself. (The doorman doesn't have much authority, and he is going to try to keep anybody out that he thinks might cause problems. Tell him who you are. Tell him you're a Christian and you want to come into his club once in a while and talk with the dancers or the bartenders or some of the patrons to share Jesus Christ with them. Let him know that you really want to help people. Give him your phone number and tell him that any time anybody needs help they can give you a call and you'll be willing to do whatever you can for them.

I have pastored in Nevada, and have worked on Sunset Strip in Hollywood for years, and most of the nightclubs that operated in the area would let me come in and talk to the people. I never pretend that I approve of what they're doing. I let them know that basically I'm opposed to it, but I love them and I love the people.

"I hope we'll see you close," I tell the manager right off, "but until you do I want to be able to come in and share Christ with you and help in any way I can." Then I ask if he has received Christ as his Saviour and I witness to him as I feel led by the Lord. When I leave I always thank him and tell him that the next time I drop in I'll give him a holler. You have to be polite and respectful. If you're going to go into a man's place of business you can't constantly create havoc or he won't let you come back.

When you have the owner's okay, you go in and start talking to the doorman. Or you sit down on a stool and introduce yourself to the bartender and tell him why you're there. Sometimes he'll offer you a coke or something. I don't drink any alcoholic beverages, but I'll accept a coke if he offers it. I turn to the person sitting by me and hand him a tract or a sticker. Usually he'll say, "What is this?" and that gives me a wide-open opportunity to explain to him what it is, and to talk about Jesus Christ.

This is the way you begin to develop a very personal ministry inside the nightclubs. Before long the people who come to the club get to know you. When you walk in they say, "Oh, no! Here comes the preacher again!" People will come over to you and ask if you're really a preacher, or a Christian, and then you just begin to share Christ.

In nightclub witnessing, you have to be able to concentrate on talking to the individual, no matter what is going on around you. I never had to adjust to that kind of environment when I began my night-life ministry because I went to many bars and nightclubs with my dad when I was just a child—from four to thirteen years old. I was never afraid of losing my reputation by entering these places because I knew that in order to work for Christ I needed to be insulated, not isolated from the world.

When I'm inside the nightclubs I don't attack the drinking and dancing and things I'm opposed to. Certainly if anybody asks me I tell them how I feel, but basically I try to avoid that. Most of the people there know their guilt; they know deep down it's wrong, and what they need is to know how to have victory through Christ in their lives. So you should deal with the person's relationship to Christ, not primarily with getting him to quit, because his main problem is not the drinking but the fact that he is lost and needs to be saved. When he has given his heart to Jesus Christ he won't need to drink, and he can walk out of the bar a completely new person.

So you begin the nightclub ministry by establishing a personal rapport with as many people as you can, all the time sharing Christ with them. In a nightclub I never talk about anything but Jesus. You don't just go in and sit down and chew the rag about any subject in the world. Your whole reason for being there is to talk about one subject—that person's salvation and his relationship with Christ.

Sometimes I've even been able to have the whole club. For a while, I preached on Sunset Strip in Bill Gazzarri's Hollywood-A-Go-Go, a well-known hangout for teen-agers. I began by asking Bill what was his lowest night. I told him I believed I could pack it every week on that night if he would give me two hours. At first, he refused to consider it, but I was stubborn; I refused to give up. Finally, he agreed to try it. I signed up several top gospel singing groups. We had gospel singing and testimonies, and then I would preach. It was so crowded that all of the people couldn't get into the building, and I did this not just once but for weeks before we got our own place on the Strip. The manager charged a door fee just as usual, so he was getting his money, and we were getting the gospel out. Although Bill had begun by throwing me out when I first asked him to let me preach, he ended up begging me to come back again. And later, when I was arrested for witnessing on the street it was Bill who put up bail for me.

I preached for almost two years off and on in nightclubs in Hollywood and in different church-front organizations like the Electric Church, which was a homosexual nightclub. It was constituted as a church, but it was really just a club, with drinking, dancing, and everything. They had a little room with a few statues, and in order to keep their license they had to have an ordained preacher come in and preach every once in a while.

They told me they needed someone, and they were about to get some other preacher who didn't even believe in God to come in and say something. But they said, "We really like you. We've heard you preach, and we saw you on television. Would you come in and preach for us once in a while?"

So I became their substitute preacher. I would come in on Sunday morning at about five o'clock, and they would unplug the jukebox and say, "Anybody that leaves while this guy is preaching will be out permanently."

Then I would get up and preach. I didn't compromise a thing in my message. I preached the full gospel, telling them how they could be delivered and set free, and sharing what Jesus could do.

They knew I wasn't homosexual. If some people who knew me said, "Well, Arthur is going down to preach in a homosexual nightclub," I couldn't worry about whether or not they thought I was gay. I was more interested in reaching these people, and I have seen the homosexuals that have been converted set free by the power of Jesus. By making myself available I took advantage of a strange type of opportunity.

I was friends with the people in the homosexual nightclubs, but I didn't compromise because of my association with them. I just went ahead and preached the gospel and the fullness of His power.

Once I was invited to be a judge of a topless contest in one of the nightclubs in Hollywood. I refused. They tried to persuade me by promising that after I got through I could say a few words. But I said it would compromise my convictions to judge a topless contest, and I wouldn't preach under those circumstances.

I told them, "No, if you'll just let me get up and preach, fine,

but I won't be a judge for a topless competition. I would judge
them all wrong, because I'd say none of them is a winner. They
all need to be saved and get right with God."

That night, at the club where the contest was held, the emcee
said, "We asked Arthur Blessitt to be a judge and he turned us
down, but we want him to come up here and take about five or
ten minutes to talk to us, anyway."

So I still got to preach, but now it was on a different basis.
They knew I wasn't there condoning what they were doing. I
was there sharing about Jesus, not compromising my faith and
my convictions.

Now, suppose you're going to have a rally in a bar or a nightclub or at a rock concert or someplace. Don't just walk in with a
bunch of straight Christians that will stand back goggle-eyed at
what's going on and not even mix and mingle with the people.
The whole idea is to meet as many of the people as you can. Remember that this is their place and you're there to reach them, so
be friendly. Go around sharing about Christ to as many people
as you can instead of just standing in a little knot over in the
corner looking on. Remember, it's a lot better to be insulated
than isolated; Jesus didn't call us to be isolated from the world,
but to be insulated against sin.

If your goal is to close the club down, the best way to do it is
to lead the owner to the Lord. This has happened all across the
United States. The owner has been converted, closed his place,
and opened it again as a Christian nightclub.

But if you don't get the owner converted you need to start
trying to close him down in another direction. One way is to rent
an adjoining building. Then you get dedicated Christians to
stand out front witnessing and singing and praying until the customers will go to another place rather than go into one where
they're constantly embarrassed.

When we started witnessing outside His Place, our Sunset
Strip gospel nightclub, business began falling off at the Session
nightclub next-door. In fact, they lost so many customers that
they finally had to close. The owner was furious with me. He said
I had cost him $75,000. Christians have now taken over there.
There is soda instead of booze, Jesus-singing instead of go-go
girls, and the place is called RIGHT ON TO JESUS.

In New York City, when we had the blitz there in Times Square, we rented a building right near a topless nightclub on Forty-fifth Street. Their sign said, TOPLESS, and there was a peephole where people could look in. On the front of our building we put, TOTALLY NAKED, and we had a peephole too. When anyone looked in, he saw a sign that said: NAKED YOU STAND BEFORE GOD, and a mirror so he could see himself. There were also some Scripture verses. You can imagine the shock!

What you try to do is administer a shock treatment to the customers going into the adjoining place. In just about every place around the country where a Christian ministry has operated next to a nightclub over a long period of time the nightclub has gone out of business.

Of course, you don't have to have a building in order to close a club. You can simply station people outside the club, witnessing, singing, praying, and passing out tracts and stickers. This should be kept up constantly. It is better to have a few pickets all night than to have a lot for thirty minutes, because many people just won't go into a nightclub if there are girls outside carrying signs that read: DO YOU WANT YOUR DAUGHTER TOPLESS AND NUDE? or WOULD YOU LIKE YOUR DAUGHTER TO BE A GO-GO DANCER? This embarrasses people so that many times they just refuse to go into the club.

When you begin to cut off money the owner's pocketbook begins to feel the pinch. You can literally picket a club to death, but you have to be able to continue as long as necessary, and it has to be an every night thing.

### Handling Problems With the Law

When you witness you should always make sure you stand about ten feet from the door, at either side, leaving plenty of room for people to walk in and out. If you start crowding up the sidewalk you can be arrested. In some places the clubs have tremendous pressure with the police, and the police may say you're blocking the sidewalk and tell you to move completely out of the way. But if there is plenty of room you should refuse. You have the right to stand on the sidewalk and witness for Christ, and you must not relinquish that right, because you're not violating any law. If just one or two of you are standing there talking to a few people, you don't have to obey anybody who orders you to leave. (Of course, you don't have the right to totally block the sidewalk so that other people can't get by.)

If you are arrested, try to get the names of any witnesses who saw you. Sometimes if you are alone, it's best just to go ahead and move on and then come back later with people who can witness your arrest so they can testify in court. It is tragic to say, but many times even the police will lie about how many people were gathered around listening to you, because the pressure is from high up to make you move on.

I found this out when I was arrested in Hollywood for committing a no more serious "crime" than standing quietly on an uncrowded sidewalk discussing Christ with two interested people. When I was told to move on I refused. I was arrested and thrown into jail. But if the police had thought of silencing me by putting me away, they soon found out that being in jail gave me a wonderful opportunity to talk about Christ to people who needed Him badly—on both sides of the bars!

When I began to read from my Bible, one of the officers took it from me. But I was not to be turned off that easily, so I began singing hymns and quoting Scripture. When they found that they couldn't keep me quiet by telling me to shut up, they let me have my Bible back if I'd stop singing. Then I began preaching to the prisoners. I found it was easier to get the message across to the men behind the bars than to those in front of them. I loved to preach on how to be happy in jail—in a twenty-foot cell the sinners can't get away from me!

Once you take a stand you can never back away from it because of possible unpleasant consequences. In other words, if you know you're right you can't compromise or change that deep, solid commitment to defend your convictions, even if it means that you might have to spend the rest of your life in jail!

Always try to prevent arrest if you can. Don't get arrested for standing in the door of somebody's building, for instance. Don't get arrested for refusing to leave a man's establishment if you're ordered to do so. Don't get arrested for putting up a sticker if a policeman says not to do it. On the other hand, as I said before, don't be afraid of arrest. If you're obsessed with fear, the effectiveness of your witness will be limited.

If it does happen, even then you need to keep your attitude pleasant. Don't stand there cursing the police and calling them names, but smile and go with them willingly, all the while looking for opportunities to witness. In the car on the way to the jail you can sing about Jesus. When they book you, you can witness to everybody there. And when you get in the jail there are lots of opportunities.

I have been in jail several times, and every time I've preached. You just ask the people in your cell if they'll let you preach and then begin talking about Jesus' power to set them free, even in a jail cell, by changing their lives. You can lead some singing, too. Try to keep your Bible if the authorities will let you. But in case they take it away, you should have enough Scripture memorized that you can quote the Bible instead of reading from it.

When a person is jailed, he is allowed to make a couple of phone calls. One of these calls should be to a friend so that someone who may be able to help will know what has happened. Use the other call to contact the best radio station or newspaper in town, to get the word out about your arrest and why you were arrested.

## COFFEE HOUSES (GOSPEL NIGHTCLUBS)

This is a very great opportunity for witnessing. I operated a gospel nightclub for four years on the Sunset Strip in Hollywood. It has become a mold for building others around the world.

We rented a building in the heart of the Strip, surrounded by go-go clubs, discotheques, teen-age dance halls, bars, homosexual clubs, and shops. Tens of thousands of young people walked the streets nightly. There was no Christian witness at all on the streets and with the people. There was the need of sharing Jesus, food, clothes, counseling, help for runaway young people, drug addicts, etc. The need for a Jesus witness at night was terrific. Shake Hollywood and the world will shake—this has proven TRUE!

We were open all night, and an average of from five hundred

to two thousand a night came in. We had colored lights, low tables, free food, coffee, and clothes.

We charged no admission and had a stage where anyone could sing quietly. Each night at midnight we had preaching and singing with an open invitation for people to come and kneel at the altar for prayer. There we counseled those who came until real victory had been won.

We have seen thousands saved inside His Place. Our biggest problem came from the society around us—the police, the clubs, the businessmen, and the churches. They opposed us for letting any person come in. We considered His Place a place to win the lost to Jesus and minister to the needs of those on the streets. We refused to let Christians just come in and sit around; we sent them out on the streets witnessing. Too many Christians sitting around would drive off the unsaved. All of our staff did personal witnessing all the time. We saved an average of from five to fifty each night. We had no dancing, smoking, or petting and asked the kids not to bring dope or liquor in. Yet the crowds always came. We handled our own problems with troublemakers and avoided calling the police at almost any price.

People desperately need a place to go at night; too often we in the church have forgotten this need. Every city needs a free all-night ministry where people can come, relax, and receive the message of Jesus. We never stop giving a direct witness for Jesus in seeking converts. Oftentimes, places like this become only gathering places for the young but lose their emphasis on winning souls to Jesus.

Some coffee houses operate only on weekends and some only one day a week. The need in a community or church may be to provide a place for Christian kids to come and enjoy a date or bring an unsaved friend. Our gospel nightclub on the strip was not just a place for a couple of young people to have a quiet Christian date!

One careful warning: Don't let the place become a hangout for a small group of "holy" Christians looking down on outsiders and rejecting the very people needing to be reached.

p.s. If your gospel nightclub starts truly reaching troublemaking drug addicts and draws crowds of young people, you can count on determined efforts to close you down! Do not be afraid to stand firm in Christian love.

# Jesus Marches

Among the most effective things in my own ministry have been Jesus marches. One of the first—if not the first—Jesus marches ever held was the one we had on Sunset Strip back in 1968. I was also in marches in 1969 and 1970, and many more in 1971. From December 25, 1969 to July 18, 1970, we walked all the way across the country carrying a cross, and we had march after march in many of the cities we went to.

Yes, I'm very familiar with marches, and I consider them one of the best means of witnessing to an area. Many times we received front-page coverage in the newspaper and substantial coverage on television—locally, statewide, and even nationally—in some of the tremendous marches we had. Don't be afraid of publicity if the purpose is to glorify God and share His message.

A Jesus march can catch the attention of a city, perhaps as nothing else can. And it's just as successful in a small town as in a big city—sometimes more so—because in a town that has only one newspaper and one radio station a march will make the front page and be an important item of local news on radio. Besides the people in the town where the march takes place, everybody in the surrounding counties will know about it, too.

A march provides a means of preaching the gospel of Christ to thousands of people in a very brief time, with a minimum of effort. It's a tremendous way of calling attention to what's going on for Jesus, and it necessitates no expense at all. It's mainly just a matter of organizing the march and getting the people together.

One of the keys to a successful march is to have a group of people who really love Jesus and are excited about it. You may need to contact other Christian groups in the area to be sure of at least a nucleus of committed Christians you can count on. But basically I think it works best if you invite everybody who would like to join in.

Don't try to get a lot of committees working on it. When that

approach is used, too many times people get to arguing and
fussing. The best way is just to decide that you need a march and
where and when you want to have it, and then invite everyone to
participate. If you do that, you won't have a lot of people com-
peting for parts on the program or wrangling about who's going
to do what. Everybody can just join in on the beautiful experience of marching for Jesus through a city.

Some preparations must be made, though, if the march is to
be a success. For one thing, if you march in the street you must
have permission from the police department. (This usually takes
several days to get.) You do not need a permit for sidewalk
marches, and there are no restrictions for them as long as you
don't have more than three, or preferably two abreast, depending
on the width of the sidewalk. Either way, you should alert the
police and let them know what you're going to do. If you do this,
and obey all the traffic signals, you cannot be prevented from
marching.

How do you know whether to march in the street or on the
sidewalk? Normally, it depends on how big a crowd you expect,
and also what you're trying to accomplish. If you have a small
group you're probably better off going down the sidewalk, where
you can contact people by giving them Jesus tracts, papers, stickers, etc. In the street, you'll have little contact with people.

### Marshals

You should have marshals, wearing arm bands to make them
easily identifiable. Their responsibilities include:

● Keeping the marchers in line in the form that has been
decided on—in two or three or four, or however many are supposed to be marching side by side.

● Stopping the marchers at red lights and DON'T WALK signs
and rushing them across when the signals change.

● Leading songs and Jesus cheers as the group marches
along. It's much more effective to be cheering and singing. If
you march in silence, too many people simply won't know you're
coming and won't see you as you go by. Songs and cheers can
show enthusiasm and attract attention without being boisterous
or smart-alecky.

● Directing the marchers and making sure police orders are obeyed. (In a big parade, a few of the marshals should be given bullhorns for use in helping to control the crowds in case there are any problems.)

● Preventing trouble. Sometimes an onlooker may start to cause trouble, maybe by assaulting somebody in the march. If that happens, the marshals should move in and stand between the attacker and whomever is being attacked. They shouldn't attack the person or hit him, but just place their bodies between him and whomever he's trying to hit. The number one thing is not to have the people stop. If the marshals keep the march moving, before long the police will see what is happening, and they will come over and take care of the situation.

### Banners and Signs

Another thing to be done before the march is to arrange for the signs the group will carry. Any time you plan a march you should get a group of Christians together and prepare an enormous number of signs to give to the people that come. The marchers should also be encouraged to bring their own, but you will almost certainly need more.

Why provide signs? Well, some people will fail to make their signs, or they'll forget to bring them. And sometimes people will bring in signs that are more political than spiritual. If nobody else showed up with any signs you might end up with only political signs and no Jesus signs at all. Then it would look like a political march for a certain issue, which of course would defeat your purpose for that particular march. Now if you had two hundred Jesus signs and ten political signs people could overlook it, but don't take a chance on having your march taken over by any group that might move in with a lot of signs that don't fit the spirit of the march.

It's a good idea to have a very expressive banner, or a cross, to be carried in front of the march. This helps to identify it immediately and lets onlookers know what you're doing. As soon as people see a march some of them inevitably react in a negative way; but when they see it's for Jesus they're less likely to stir up any trouble.

### Medical Services

If you have a large march, be sure to make arrangements with the American Red Cross or some other organization to have a group of volunteer nurses and doctors available. It's always possible that someone might fall or get hurt in some way, and medical help would also be needed quickly in case of heat exhaustion, a heart attack, or some other emergency.

On a hot day, water should be provided somewhere along the route—not for everyone to stop for a drink, but so that somebody who is really exhausted can get a cool drink and rest.

### Time and Place

Timing is important. If possible, plan to conduct the march early in the day so that news reporters can cover it and still be able to prepare their stories in time for the evening news. If you have a march at five in the afternoon there's no way it can make the evening news reports—either in the papers, on radio, or TV. However, if you have it at one in the afternoon there's a much better chance of coverage.

Try to plan your march to go by some point of significance. When we marched in New York City, for example, we marched right down Forty-second Street at Times Square. Had we marched down Forty-third Street it wouldn't have excited nearly as much interest, and the news coverage would almost certainly have been much less. We selected Forty-second Street because it is famous for its pornographic bookstores and exploitation of sex.

In Hollywood, you could march down Santa Monica Boulevard and nobody would pay much attention. But if you march down Sunset Strip, it's another story. If you march down a back street in Chicago it doesn't matter, but a march to the Civic Center on Michigan Avenue would be significant. If you march for Jesus in Washington, D.C., from the Department of Agriculture to the Department of Health, Education, and Welfare, that's not much of a march, but if you march past the White House or the Capitol or the Washington Monument you have something that people can identify, and the march is more likely to make news.

### *Distance*

How far should you march? Don't make the mistake of turning it into an endurance test. I was in one march that had been planned to go for fifteen miles. It was after dark before we came to our destination. It was cold too, and the reporters and everyone else had left. The marchers were exhausted, and a lot of the kids had blisters on their feet. So, while it was a joyful time, it lost most of its impact because it was just too long.

From a mile to a maximum of three miles is sufficient for the accomplishment of the purpose. Always remember that a march shouldn't be a test of physical stamina, but a demonstration of the commitment of the individuals to Jesus Christ.

### *Size*

As for the size of the march, I think it can't be stressed too much that the numbers don't necessarily have anything to do with its impact. That's not true in every case, though. For instance, a march may appear insignificant if you're having it right down the main street of a huge city and you only have a few people. The press probably won't consider it big enough to matter, and you're not likely to get any coverage.

But many times a small march—one with only fifty or seventy-five people—can accomplish a lot. In Van Nuys, California, a small group of not more than seventy-five young people from one church marched on New Year's Eve around some nude nightclubs, and that made news. The timing helped, since it was New Year's Eve, and the clubs actually had to close down.

Our marches on Sunset Strip, some with only a couple of hundred people, made news because other marches in the same area had ended in riots, and to have a march that ended peacefully was news.

The march I mentioned that we had through Times Square in New York City involved only about three hundred young people. But it was so well covered because of where it was, who those young people were, and what they were doing in Times Square.

So don't just be hung up on numbers. And whatever you do, don't ever try to impress the news media by giving a big estimate of size that you may not be able to live up to. It's much better to be honest than it is to try to impress them with an inflated figure, because once they get there they're going to see how many there are anyway. Besides—and even more important—they just don't expect a Christian to try to manipulate figures.

### Points of Assembly and Dispersal

You can minimize problems of gathering the marchers together and getting them home afterwards by selecting assembly and dispersal points that are near public transportation and easy to reach by car. They should both be places where it is possible to talk to the group and have a little music. Before the march begins it's good to have some singing practice; try a few cheers, and share the excitement of what is going to happen. Then, when the marshals give the signal, the group files out and begins the march.

### Destination

The destination should be well publicized in advance. When the group arrives there, plan to have a little music, if possible, but keep it short. If you have a long music program at the end you usually lose most of the people who have joined you during the march. I would say that the music period should be not more than ten minutes long. Following the music, you can have a speaker who will share the message of Christ and give an invitation. Then Christians from your group should be ready to counsel a lot of people that make decisions for Christ. You should also appoint someone to act as spokesman, giving a clear statement of purpose and answering questions from reporters or other interested individuals.

# Witnessing at Special Events

## SHOPPING CENTER RALLIES

Usually, shopping center rallies are very effective, and they can draw tremendous crowds. On the other hand, the people may not dig it at all, and then maybe no one, or only a very few, will come over. I've been in shopping center rallies that drew thousands. By putting on a good, really interesting program it may be that you can reach more unchurched people at one rally than the normal church does in two or three years. I've seen hundreds of people saved in these rallies, and I think the opportunities are tremendous.

Before you begin planning your rally, it's normally best to meet with the management of the shopping center. Of course, you can sometimes just go out and set up a rally without talking to anyone. I have done this, but there's always the risk of having the manager or someone who works for him come out and ask you to leave. (They generally won't try to arrest you, but if you don't go when they tell you to they might.)

So, while it's true that you can sometimes pull off a rally at a shopping center by just doing it without asking anybody, it's usually best to get permission, at least from one store. If one store manager will give you permission to meet in front of his place of business, the others usually won't object.

Your meeting is more likely to succeed if it is well publicized. One good way to do this is to put out handbills in the area. You can also go to the ice-cream stands and places where the kids hang out and tell them about it. Another way is to promote the rally in churches around the area and ask their people to come out. At some shopping centers there's a public address system that covers all the stores. A lot of times you can get your rally promoted in that way.

If you're in an enclosed shopping center with a mall inside you may be able to have a rally inside the mall. In that case, you can plug right into their public address system and just broadcast into all of the stores. Of course, this is extremely effective.

You should arrange to have a truck—maybe a flatbed or a pickup—that will provide a raised place for your people to stand. Get together a good singing group, and when they start singing, hopefully a crowd will begin to gather.

Members of your team should be at the shopping center at least an hour ahead of time, talking to the people about Jesus and inviting them to the rally. If it's a big, crowded place, sometimes a rally will draw enough people just by the very fact that it's there. But other times you really need to bring a good number of your own people in to give you a base upon which to build.

The big secret is in getting out where the people are and providing something they're interested in. To get the right results, it must be done in good taste. Make it clear that you're not cramming anything down people's throats, but you've got a message to share—something they want to know.

## STREET PREACHING

This form of witness really tells you where it's at, because if a street preacher isn't hitting the points right the people aren't going to stay around—or if they do stay it will be to argue and fuss and not to listen to him. In church, people don't usually get up and walk out, but no one is committed to stay and listen to a street preacher, so he really has to have something to say.

Many of the street preaching meetings I've seen haven't been as effective as they should have been, simply because the preacher behaved as though he hated everybody that he was preaching to, and that's the wrong impression to give. A street preacher ought to show love and compassion, and make it very clear that he has something everybody should be interested in.

I've preached on the streets since I was just a kid. The most effective street preaching ministry I ever had was in Times Square in New York, at Forty-seventh St. and Broadway. It was in the old Duffy Square, a small triangle in the midst of all the congestion, with tens of thousands of people milling around. We were in this kind of isolated spot, right in the middle of this jungle of people, and we would get a group of Christians—maybe ten or forty or fifty—and sit down in a circle and begin to play guitars and sing. Crowds would gather around during the hour-and-a-half rally; we averaged two or three thousand a night. We would sing and have testimonies in between the songs, and then I would preach and give an invitation. It was one of the most tremendous things I've witnessed anywhere.

As I've already said, street preaching needs to be sharing something, not preaching at people, and there should be good singing, not singing at people. I think this is why our New York street ministry was so effective. As we sat together, singing with each other, the people felt that they were looking in on something we were enjoying. Instead of seeming to say, "We have something we all want you to hear," we seemed to be saying, "We have something we are enjoying; wouldn't you like to enjoy it with us?" The crowds literally swarmed to us. There were so many people that a lot of them actually couldn't see us; nevertheless, they stayed to listen because there was something there they really wanted to hear.

The street preacher and the people helping him should have good material to give to the people who pass by or stop. And you should all be geared to the need for dealing personally with individuals, not just putting on a program and then walking away. As soon as you get through preaching, turn around to the people and begin to talk with them, one by one. If possible, your preaching should be done on a regular basis, so that people will know they can come out and find you there and hear you preach at a certain time.

Those who are out street preaching should never argue with any heckler who tries to raise a question. In other words, if you're preaching—preach. If you stop to answer questions or respond to taunts, it will almost certainly deteriorate into just a yelling session.

And you should never get angry with anybody, no matter how they heckle you. Keep a firm grip on your self-control. If the hecklers get so bad you can't ignore them, just quietly kneel and pray with your group, thereby demonstrating greater understanding than you would if you allowed yourself to become involved in a fight.

The meetings we had in Duffy Square were street preaching,

but they weren't held literally on the street, because we had an area where people could gather. Now, had we been doing this on the sidewalk, (once we blocked the sidewalk and people started walking out in the street) the police would have had to ask us to leave in order to keep the people from getting hit by cars. Many times street preaching creates this kind of problem, especially if the preacher is really drawing a crowd.

If you run into trouble with the police, many times you can find an unused area where you can continue your ministry. A gas station owner whose place is closed at night might let you use his parking lot, for example, or you might get permission to use some other property that is near the sidewalk, but not actually on it, so that the people can stand on private property while you're preaching.

You can always just go ahead and street preach until you do run into a problem, but if you expect to draw a big crowd it's better to go ahead and find some place to stand where you won't create congestion.

## BEACH RALLIES

A beach rally can be fantastic. You can put one on with no more than ten kids with guitars, say around eleven in the morning when crowds are on the beach. The group can stir up interest by fanning out and passing out tracts and at the same time telling everyone that there will be singing in a certain place in fifteen minutes. But even if you don't do that people will generally come up when you begin to sing.

As the crowd gathers around to hear what's going on, your group will sing and maybe have a testimony or two and then sing some more. Then somebody else will get up and testify about Jesus, and you'll ask everyone to bow and pray and invite them to give their hearts to Christ. You can ask those who will do that to come up to the front and acknowledge their commitment, or have them just lift their hands, wherever they happen to be, and one of the Christians in your group can go sit down by them and share his love for Christ. You should have a supply of Bibles to give out to these new converts.

Then, when you finish with that group, you can just move down the beach several hundred yards and do another one, and so on. That way, you can speak to thousands of people in one day, with nothing but a few guitars and a handful of kids who are turned on to Jesus.

If you use amplifiers you may have to have a permit. Amplifiers can almost guarantee that you'll draw a crowd if you have a pretty good music group singing good songs. But many times it's just as effective to have a spontaneous rally. That is what I've done most often. You just start with maybe ten kids and you sit down and begin playing guitars and singing and clapping, and before long a whole crowd of people will gather around.

Most of the time there are very few problems with beach rallies. I have been at beach rallies all around the country, and the response is marvelous; it's the same from coast to coast. Especially during the holiday season, and all during the summer, too, there are just millions of people going to the beach. Some are bored. Some are lonely. And almost all are looking for something to do.

## ROCK CONCERTS

If a rock concert is being held in town you can talk to the promoter or to the manager of one of the groups and just say, "Hey, during one of the band changes how about giving me five minutes to get up and speak and share about Christ? The kids need some spiritual lift, so how about letting me share with them?"

In this way I've preached before Steppenwolf, Jefferson Airplane, Janis Joplin, Jimi Hendrix—all kinds of music groups—just simply by asking for an opportunity to speak before their group came on or between the bands. It's fantastic! You really don't know what you can do. There's no limit—unless you've been defeated already in your mind.

I was the first preacher ever to preach at a rock festival. At the West Palm Beach international festival back in 1969 we had a Jesus tent that distributed Bibles and bags of free food. Inside the bags with the food were gospel tracts. In this way we helped meet the needs—both physical and spiritual—of as many kids as we could.

I have preached to over a million kids at rock festivals and rock concerts alone. First, I would speak and have an invitation to prayer. Then I would invite those who made a commitment to

Christ to come back to our Jesus tent, where we had counselors who were able to talk with them.

If you have a physical ministry, as well as a spiritual ministry—providing food or blankets or whatever you can to help the physical needs of the kids—you can combine this in a very meaningful way with your prime objective, which should always be to share the gospel of Jesus Christ. Because of the crowds an event of this kind draws, you have a fantastic opportunity to witness to tens of thousands of kids that otherwise would never be reached with the gospel.

## JESUS FESTIVALS

You can put on your own Christian rock concert by getting a folk-rock Jesus singing group to give a concert at the band shell or at a park or beach in your city, maybe on a Saturday afternoon. With good music and testimonies, this can be a tremondous outreach.

## SPORTS EVENTS

You can often get permission to witness during an intermission or at half-time in basketball games or football games, or between innings at baseball games. One way to do this kind of witnessing is to go up and speak from the announcing booth, or you can drive out on the field in a pickup truck and use the back of the truck for your platform.

You may be able to tie your appearance into something that's going on. If you're having a special rally in town, you might introduce the speaker and invite everyone to come. Or, if there's a political campaign you might want to refer to that. But don't waste your opportunity on a bunch of personality acknowledgments. God has given you a few minutes, so take advantage of the time and speak up boldly for Him. Still another way to get attention is to lead off with an exciting illustration. But don't just get up and tell an irrelevant joke. In fact, don't tell a joke at all. If you've got to have humor, tell a living experience that is humorous. The important thing is to be excited. You may get only three or four minutes, but you can witness to thousands of people during that short time.

Always be careful not to exceed your time limit. Even if you're given only two minutes, don't speak for more than the allotted time. Never underestimate what God can do through you, even in a very brief time.

Another way to witness at sports events is to stand around the concession booths distributing material and witnessing for Christ. You can do the same type of thing at political rallies, demonstration marches, and the like.

Or you can get a group together and agree on what section you'll sit in. You might all want to carry signs with you, which you can keep out of sight, maybe by hiding them under your coats. Then, during a slow spot you can all pull out your signs and begin to do Jesus cheers. Your group can go out through the area where the game is being played, blitzing the crowd with Jesus papers, gospel tracts, and stickers.

I've preached in arenas before and after wrestling matches simply by convincing the promoter that it would be a novel idea, that the people would probably dig it, and that he would get a lot of news coverage out of it. It doesn't matter if you have to sell the man by making him see that letting you speak will be so novel that there'll be all kinds of publicity. Don't hesitate to stress the publicity angle, because you know the kind of news that comes out will acknowledge the Lord.

Now, don't ever let yourself get trapped in a situation where your witness will not be a clear-cut stand for Jesus. For one thing, don't take any money for it. It must be absolutely clear that you're going in as a Christian trying to win these people to Christ. You don't have to pretend to condone what is going on, because you may be totally opposed to it. Simply go in on the basis that you want to share the positive message of Jesus Christ.

I repeat, don't ever underestimate what God can help you do. Sometimes, in ways you would never dream, He will reach out and lend a helping hand if you have faith and don't give up.

Here's an example of what happened to me. I was out of money, and sixty dollars in rent had to be paid the next day. As I went from bar to bar witnessing, I racked my brain for some way to get that money, but there just seemed to be no way. Then, in one of the bars where I stopped, I saw a drunk burn a one-hundred-dollar bill. I began to talk to him, hoping to bring him to Christ. In a fit of drunken irrationality, he tried to get me to take a handful of his money, but I refused, telling him he couldn't buy me. After a while, he tried again. "God has told me to give you this money," he said. This time I took it. When I got home, I found that it amounted to exactly sixty dollars.

## STREET BLITZES

To put on a street blitz, you get a group of people together, from five to thirty or even more, and you go downtown, or in a big city you would take a certain number of streets. Just a few teams can look like a lot of people. Only fifteen or twenty people, spread out over an area, can look like a whole lot more.

I call it a blitz because you hit an area intensively, and you do it again and again. Suddenly you just appear on the scene, and you keep going back for several days, or maybe every night for a long time.

Before going out, you meet with the group and give them simple instructions on how to lead a person to Jesus Christ. Talk with them on counseling and dealing with individuals who want to be saved. Hand out supplies of Bibles, gospel tracts, and other materials you plan to distribute. Divide up into teams of two and assign a time when you're going to come back to the meeting place for prayer.

Then you go out on the streets. With the members of your group, all in pairs, you stand at corners giving out tracts and stickers to people passing by. As you do this, you smile and say "Jesus loves you," or "God bless you." If a person pauses, you ask him if he has received Christ, and you begin a witness right there on the spot.

After you have witnessed for a while in this way, you can get together again and go singing down the sidewalks playing guitars, doing Jesus cheers, and stopping to talk to people along the way. This is not really an official march, but in a sense it is because you're going along as a group having a marvelous time for Christ in the downtown area.

# Witnessing Day by Day

## BUSES, AIRPLANES, TRAINS

When you're traveling, you can find all kinds of opportunities to talk to people about Jesus. I have stood up on a crowded bus and said, "Would anybody who doesn't want to hear me preach and talk to you about Jesus just raise your hand or tell me you don't want to hear me, and I won't preach. But unless someone objects I'd like to preach to you." (I started out that way to let them know I wasn't trying to force it on them if they didn't want to hear.) If no one objected, I just went ahead and preached on the bus, and I was able to lead some of the people to Jesus.

Sometimes on an airplane I have felt led to witness, and when I got to my seat I'd stand up and say, "Friends, if any of you want to talk about Jesus Christ, I'm a Christian and I'd love to talk with you. Feel free to come and sit down with me." During the flight, people would come back and talk, and some of them made the decision to give their lives to Christ.

Nowadays, almost every time I'm on an airplane I wait outside until the last person is aboard and then as I go onto the plane I give the stewardess a Jesus sticker and a tract, and as I go down the aisle I start passing out tracts and stickers to each person. I make my way all the way to the back and sit down, and after the plane takes off all kinds of people come back to where I am and say things like, "What do you mean by this?" or "I've looked this over, and I'm interested." It's a fine way to witness.

One day when I was on an airplane the stewardess announced, just before we were about to take off, "In case of emergency . . . . " I hollered, "Pray." She came back and said, "Young man would you *please* restrain yourself." Another time a stewardess asked me what my final destination was. I told her, "Heaven!" She almost dropped her chart!

41

Suppose you're at an airport, a bus terminal, or a railroad station and you've got two hours between flights. You can use that time to go around passing out tracts or putting them in the magazine racks. Or you can just blitz the whole place by sticking Jesus stickers everywhere—along the walkways, in the restrooms, etc. Or you might go around and witness to other travelers, or just walk down the streets talking to people about Jesus.

## BOWLING ALLEYS, SKATING RINKS

Sometimes, I have gone down to a bowling alley and asked the manager if I could take five minutes and share the message of Jesus Christ, and I've been given that opportunity. I've also spoken at skating rinks. It's a real thrill to have people skate up and give their hearts to Jesus! In bowling alleys I like to preach on rolling for Jesus.

## GAS STATIONS

There are many business places you can witness in. With a little concentration, you can find all kinds of opportunities. Just for an example, take gas stations.

A gas station visit can mean more than simply tanking up with gas. It can give you the occasion to witness to the attendant and to leave tracts where they'll be picked up by other people who come to the station. You can actually have a mission at that station instead of just filling up your car.

When you drive in, don't just say, "Fill it up," but say, "God bless you, sir," or "Jesus loves you, sir. I'd like you to fill it up." While he is filling up your car you can go into the rest room and put red stickers and gospel tracts there. It's kind of far out, but you might even unroll the toilet tissue and put little red Jesus stickers along it, or put in some Jesus tracts and roll it back up. As the man services your car you can talk to him about Jesus, and just before you give him the credit card or money be sure to give him a gospel tract.

Can you imagine what would happen if every Christian did that every time he bought gas? The whole gas station world would either get saved, quit, or have a nervous breakdown, because every time a Christian came driving in the guy would wonder, "Is he going to buy gas or save me?" When the driver reached in his pocket, the attendant would think "Will it be a credit card or a Bible?" It couldn't help making a real impact if everywhere we went we were witnessing about our Christian faith.

## RESTAURANTS

When you're eating away from home, there are lots of ways to witness. When you enter the restaurant, you can put a Jesus sticker on the door. Then, when the waitress brings you the menu, say, "Thank you, ma'am, may I leave you something?" and you hand her a gospel tract, very politely. Inside the menu, you can stick a gospel tract and then when the next person starts to order he'll find it there. You can pull back several napkins and insert tracts and then push them all back in place. You can witness and share Christ with the waitress.

Again, you can go to the rest room and leave tracts and stickers. You can put a sticker on the bill, put one on the cash register, and give some to people you meet. You can give the waitress a bunch of stickers and tell her to give them to the other waitresses and to the cooks in the back.

A restaurant can be a tremendous mission field when you look for opportunities to approach it in that way.

## GROCERY STORES, LAUNDROMATS, DOCTORS' OFFICES

As you go about your daily routine, you can constantly witness for Christ. Here are some suggestions:

● When you grocery shop, leave gospel tracts in the store, maybe around the liquor counter, or in a six-pack of beer.

● A tremendous place to leave tracts is on the bulletin boards they have in supermarkets. You can always stick a tract up there, and people will read it. Do that every time you go shopping, and you can keep the bulletin board well supplied.

● You can say a few words for Jesus to the cashier as you leave, and to the people in front of you or behind you.

● When you're waiting around at a laundromat, you have a fantastic opportunity to witness. You can put tracts on the washing machines and the dryers. You can also bring Christian magazines and leave them lying around. This is a beautiful opportunity, because people have time on their hands while they wait, and they're likely to pick up the magazines and start reading them.

● You can do the same thing in a doctor's office. When you go to the doctor, bring along some Christian magazines and leave them in the waiting room as you go in.

## TAXIS, HOTELS, MOTELS

When you're riding in a cab, you can witness to the driver. One way is to say to him, "Man, I want to go to the fun spot in town." He'll start rapping off Lulu's Go-Go Joint and all the sin spots, and that opens the door for you to say, "You're missing out on the greatest fun in life if that's what you think fun is." Then you can start talking about Jesus Christ.

When you're registering at a hotel or motel you can put down your address and then add "Future address: Heaven." And you can write in some Christian witness right there on the form. I always do that, and many people have commented on it. It's a very sincere thing, because you're sharing a witness to the individual who is checking you in.

You can witness to the maids who take care of your room in a hotel or motel by leaving a Bible or some tracts for them, with a note saying that the things are intended for them.

## HOSPITALS, NURSING HOMES

There are many opportunities for ministry in these places. You might begin by bringing flowers and get-well cards with Scripture verses. You can also give out gospel materials, and go from room to room, cheering the sick and bearing witness to Jesus Christ.

I spent a lot of time at nursing homes when I was in college, and even now I like to stop by and minister to the older people. If you do this, though, it needs to be on a regular basis, because old people need ongoing love and fellowship, not just a one-shot visit. Many of them are sadly neglected, and it's a ripe field for evangelism.

## FACTORIES

A lot of times there are opportunities for evangelism at the lunch hour in factories. I've often spoken at plants that have Christian Bible study groups that meet at noontime. The people can eat their lunch during the service, and there's time for a short period of singing and a brief talk or a few minutes of Bible study.

# *Seeking Opportunities to Witness*

## JAILS

The first time I ever tried to preach in a jail my attempt was something less than a howling success. However, I did manage to lead one man to Jesus, out of the one hundred or so locked up together in a huge enclosure.

It happened when I was still going to college. I had heard that some of the guys were going down to the jail to preach and witness, and I decided to go along and look on. Too late, I found that I was expected to actually go in among that crowd of prisoners and try to bring them to Christ!

I began hesitantly, by announcing, in a timid voice, that I was going to preach. No one made a move to stop me; in fact, no one made any move at all. Ignoring me completely, the men kept on doing whatever they had been doing when I came in— some watching TV, some listening to the radio, some reading, but no one paying the slightest attention to me.

Finally, I decided to at least make myself heard, and I began leafing furiously through my Bible, quoting verse after verse at the top of my voice. Having caught the attention of three or four of the men, I began to preach. It wasn't much of a sermon; I faltered, I rambled, I repeated, but what my remarks lacked in quality they made up in length. Having agreed to stay in the cell for forty-five minutes, I just kept on talking.

When I had run entirely out of steam, I asked if anyone wanted to be saved. One man volunteered. Afterward, he thanked me and invited me back. I preached many times in that jail after that, and came to regard those sessions as some of the most exciting times of my whole college career.

Many prisoners in jails and juvenile delinquents in reformatories are really hungry for someone to come out and talk to them personally and bear witness to Christ. I did this for a year at the youth training school for boys in Nevada while I was a pastor in a nearby town. I'd go out every Wednesday night for Bible study and a question-and-answer session. It turned out to be a tremendous ministry.

The school housed 150 boys, all under eighteen, doing time for everything from vagrancy to murder. At our first service only one boy was saved, but soon more than half were showing up for the meetings, and during the time I was there fifty boys gave their lives to Christ. Two even decided to become preachers. One of those two had been the toughest kid in the entire school.

I encouraged the boys to attend our church. Sometimes I would take one or two of them out for a special event—a ride in the country, a picnic, or a meal. We also had some great Bible discussions after our services each week.

## FAIRS

Another outreach idea is to have a booth you can work out of at a state or county fair. You should have some interesting Christ-centered materials that you can give away, and your group can circulate around, doing personal witnessing and counseling as well. It's easy to move into a fair and distribute material and witness and share Christ all over the area.

## HIGH SCHOOLS, COLLEGES

Those of you who are still in school can help make your schools the scene of perpetual revival. As a step toward this goal, try organizing a small group of fellow students to meet daily— or every other day. You can gather in the center of the campus and sit in a circle out on the grass or on a paved area, either before or immediately after school. You don't even need permission to do this. There's really no difference between five or ten kids sitting around talking about dates, sports, or politics and the same group getting together to talk about Jesus.

You can turn these meetings into impromptu rallies by beginning some good songs, like "We're One in the Spirit, We're One in the Lord"—songs of worship that will unite the people. After a few songs you can have testimonies from different kids. Then you can sing some more, after which someone can read the Scripture and you can begin a discussion. (During this

period, be careful not to let any debates or arguments develop.)
One person can share a Bible message and then you might all
hold hands in a circle of prayer and maybe do a Jesus cheer.

At the close, you can invite those who need to receive Jesus
Christ to do so. You could ask them to raise their hands, or just
everyone turn around and ask the people around them if they
have made a commitment to Him in their hearts. To start your
group growing, suggest that the students who take part invite
fellow students to join in with them.

A Jesus march around the campus is a tremendous way of
having a witness in the school. You don't need a permit for it as
long as you're off campus and not blocking traffic, and are obey-
ing all the traffic signals. You can witness in this way at ball
games and other school activities, too, marching with cheers and
distributing tracts and materials.

You can also put gospel tracts in the school lockers or stick
Jesus stickers around the school and Jesus messages on the bulletin board, but there is a limit to how much of this you can do
in most schools.

There are a lot of things that have no restrictions at all, however. You can wear Jesus buttons and tee shirts and have Jesus
stickers on your notebooks and things like that. You can always
use expressions like "God bless you," and "Jesus loves you," and
"Praise God." These are all ways of witnessing to your friends
and classmates.

When you're preparing assignments or reports for your classes
you can often bring in gospel subjects. For instance, you could
give a report of a Jesus movement or a Christian character in
history. In speech class, you might give a testimony, fulfilling
the assignment and at the same time giving a very personal witness. If you're writing poems, they can have a Christian message.
In fact, there's almost no end to the ways you can bring the
gospel in if you try.

If you're in college, your group can sponsor interesting speak-
ers who will witness for Jesus on your campus. Many college
campuses have open forum areas. I've spoken on campus after
campus, where we would have a rally featuring a singing group.
After speaking, singing, and hearing testimonials at the student
center, we would go out and meet individual kids and share
Jesus Christ with them.

Even when other organizations are having rallies you can often witness to their groups at an appropriate time. Of course, you should remember that it is their meeting and not try to break it up or completely take over.

In the dorms, you can engage in door-to-door evangelism, just sharing the gospel of Jesus Christ with other students, giving out material, and asking people if they have received the Lord.

## IN YOUR HOME

A good way to witness right in your own home is to have a tract rack inside your front door. This is especially helpful in the city, where many salesmen and other strangers come to the door. When you open the door, you can just reach over and give the person a tract and a little of your testimony.

If friends invite you to visit them, you can carry your Bible with you. Someone is sure to comment on it, or ask a question, and you can just begin right there at the table, or wherever you happen to be, sharing Jesus Christ with them.

When someone is killed in a car accident or arrested or gets into the news in some other tragic way, the home address is often given in the papers. You can have a worthwhile ministry by writing letters to people in trouble and to families of accident victims, saying a word of consolation and sending them salvation tracts. This is a particularly good activity for elderly people, or for women who are at home all day with time on their hands.

In the course of an ordinary day, you can find lots of other opportunities to witness. For instance, I have put Jesus stickers on my oil stick and on the motor of my car, so that when anybody opens the hood to look at the motor or check the oil he looks down and sees the Word of God.

If something is wrong with your stereo and you have to get it repaired, you can take along a gospel record when you go to pick it up and play that record to see if the machine is working right.

If something goes wrong with your television and a repairman comes to your house, you can ask about his relationship with Jesus, witness to him, and give him tracts and other material.

When you get postage-paid return envelopes, don't throw them away. Instead, stick a tract inside, seal the envelope, and mail it back. Many people get hundreds of these envelopes a year, and if you return them the sender will be paying the postage and you can witness for free. I know convalescent homes where patients save up all their envelopes and once a week they have a "stuffing party," where they pray for all the people they will be witnessing to—the secretaries and others who will open the envelopes.

Every time you leave home, be sure you have plenty of gospel tracts, stickers, and other Christian materials. Then, as you go about your day's business you can witness everywhere you go by leaving a tract. In this way, many people can witness scores of times during a day.

## CALL-IN RADIO PROGRAMS, LETTERS TO EDITORS

From your home, you can also witness through the call-in programs on radio. Don't be nasty or antagonistic when you call in, just share the message of Jesus Christ in your conversation. That way you can preach to thousands of people who may be listening to that particular show who otherwise might miss the opportunity of hearing a good word for Jesus.

All sorts of pressure groups organize to call in to these programs, so why shouldn't Christians plan to take this way of bearing their testimony?

Another method of reaching out is to send letters to editors of various newspapers and magazines, carefully finding ways of witnessing for Jesus. Be sure your message is clear and polite, not narrow-minded or sarcastic. Many times this is a way to convey a beautiful witness for Jesus to a large group of people who read that particular publication.

## TELEPHONE EVANGELISM

This is another great opportunity. Many people who aren't able to get out can spend hours dialing the telephone and witnessing to people in that way. Don't beat around the bush when you talk to people on the phone. I think your approach should be a direct questioning; if you're indefinite, people wonder what you're after. But if you tell them right away why you're calling— that you're a Christian and would like to talk with them about their relationship wih Jesus Christ—this kind of telephone ministry can accomplish a lot.

When I went to Nevada to start a church it was in the middle of the winter, and my wife and I spent hours every day calling one family after another. We just went through the telephone book, sharing Christ, and when we found a family that was interested we made an appointment to go over and visit them. We led many people to Christ right on the phone.

## ON THE JOB

If you have a job, a very effective thing to do is to go out with different people each day for lunch, or to sit with various individuals in the company cafeteria so that you can share Christ with as many of your co-workers as possible. You can carry your Bible and during conversations share the message of Jesus.

## NEIGHBORHOOD OUTREACH

There's a real good opportunity in going out to mobile home courts or new housing areas. As you go from trailer to trailer or from house to house distributing gospel material, many times you'll find a Christian family that can begin a Bible study program for people in their neighborhood. Or you might want to begin Bible study groups for the children of the families.

The same kind of thing can be done in apartment building complexes, especially in some of the high-rises in poorer areas where the children may be wandering around the streets with nothing to do. You might be able to arrange to use an empty building, or meet in someone's home. Or you might just get the group together out in the back yard, with everyone sitting around on the grass. It's quite possible that you could round up fifty or more kids each time for this kind of on-the-spot Bible study, with Bible stories, singing, and picture cards for the children to take home.

## JESUS HOUSES

When people are won to Jesus from very problem-filled backgrounds, often they need immediate help in Bible study, fellowship and counsel that they can find almost nowhere else except by being in close contact with Christians that can provide it. Seeing this desperate need, we opened houses where new converts could come in and live free for a few weeks then go out on their own to live lives of victory in Jesus. We first opened one, then two, then encouraged the opening of others around the country.

These houses need strong leadership, preferably a husband and wife. There need to be general rules and responsibilities while the new Christians are there. Bible study, prayer, fellowship, and witnessing are very important.

Some of the houses are more organized than others. Some have twenty to fifty kids. Others may be run by two or three working young people who allow five or six others who need help to live with them, or by a couple who takes in two to four or five to live with them.

One should always be careful that the emphasis should be on training the new convert to go into the world and be a strong responsible witness there, rather than staying in a withdrawn isolated environment. Almost any strong Christian can open a Jesus house!

Some so-called Jesus Houses serve as a combination coffee house and Christian house. Each person with a burden should seek to find the best means to reach his own community.

## THEATER SERVICES

If you want to have a revival meeting, consider renting a downtown theater in a prime area instead of holding it in a church. Many of the people who need to be reached will come for this kind of thing when they wouldn't go to a church. A theater that is open only in the evenings will sometimes rent space for noonday services, or you might be able to rent an empty theater building for night meetings.

Why will people attend services in a theater when they wouldn't go to a church? I think one reason is that the churches are missing the boat when it comes to their basic mission of saving souls. Most churches seem to be open only a few hours a week—for Sunday services and maybe a few social gatherings on other days.

But why should their doors *ever* close? Shouldn't a person be able to find help when he needs it—not just during the hours

when churches traditionally choose to open? The refusal of
many churches to inconvenience themselves to meet the needs
of the people they should be serving has turned a lot of people
off so completely that they would never think of trying a church
when they need help.

## MASS MEDIA

Radio and television programs are other means of taking the
gospel where the people are. The most common way is to buy
time from the stations. If you do this, be careful not to let appeals for money become a prime part of your programing.
Mainly, your goal should simply be to share the message of
Christ.

Always be completely honest with your listeners and try to develop a real integrity so that you can win their trust.

If you can get on a talk show, that is fine. I've been on many
of these shows, sharing the gospel of Christ, and the number of
people that have been converted—just the ones that I know of
has been tremendous. However, the gospel spots on the air are
very effective, too.

Newspaper ads can also help spread the word. I don't mean
just advertising a church service, although that is all right, too,
but something more unusual, like putting a gospel message on
the entertainment page.

If you can find some Christians who are creative and have
good writing skills you might even want to start your own
newspaper—a Jesus paper that would carry Bible studies, gospel
messages, and Christian news of your area. Many times, the
more local the news the more interesting the newspaper is because people want to know what is happening in their own area.

## CRUSADES

A crusade featuring an interesting, dynamic speaker and tremendous music can draw as many as 25,000 people. I have
preached at hundreds of these rallies around the country, and
have found magnificent response.

In planning a program of this kind, be sure to keep it moving.
Don't let the music drag on and on or let long appeals for fi-
nances and introductions of dignitaries obscure the real purpose,

which should be to worship and share the excitement of commitment to Jesus Christ, to report what God is doing, and to present a challenge for the unsaved to receive Christ. Counseling should be given on the spot to those who make decisions for Christ.

## SOCIAL OUTCASTS

In almost every section of the country there is probably an area that has been taken over by groups like the Hell's Angels or the Black Panthers or some notorious local street gang. Maybe it's a house where a lot of dope addicts hang out, or motorcycle riders, or thugs. In other words, it's a house or camp or building that is just totally conceded to Satan.

Too often, Christians are afraid to go there. Many times, they'll drive by a place year after year, and they'll say, "That's a cat house" (house of prostitution), or "Dope addicts hang out there," but they never go in.

When I first went to a Hell's Angels camp I had read about them in a newspaper story about arrests of some of their guys, and I felt moved by God to go. I found out where the camp was and drove up in my car and blew the horn. A guy came out with a gun and asked me what I was doing there.

"I'm Arthur Blessitt," I told him. "I read about you guys in the newspaper. I'd like to be the minister to the Hell's Angels. You fellows need the Lord." He said, "No, we need a lawyer." I replied that God could work on the judge, the jury, and the police, all at the same time. He said, "You're weird enough, come on in!" I went in and talked to the bikers for about an hour. They listened without interrupting, except to ask a few questions.

Whenever you're witnessing, but especially to rough guys like bikers and gangsters, you have to confront them straight and start witnessing on a direct basis. If you beat around the bush or stutter and stammer, you may be dead. In other words, when you go to the roughest spot in town you speak right up and tell them who you are and why you're there and what you want to do.

Usually they'll start by cursing you or laughing at you or something, but you have to just stay there and punch with them.

If they laugh, you laugh and say, "Man, you can laugh better when you're saved. You'll have more to laugh about because you'll have the joy of the Lord in your heart."

If they start cursing you, just smile and say, "Brother, when you really know Him you won't feel that way about Him. You know, He loves you even while you curse Him," and then you just start sharing a face-to-face confrontation.

You don't have to try and prove how tough you are. Just let them know what Jesus has done for you, and they'll respect your guts and your commitment to Christ.

Many converts from these kinds of gangs turn out to be tremendous Christians because they're used to being totally dedicated to what they're involved in. So, when they realize that Jesus is the answer, they become totally dedicated to Him, and they make great disciples and great Christians.

You just can't ignore people like this. Whenever you see a need, no matter how uninviting the situation may seem, you have to try to meet it.

I remember one time I was asked to preach at the funeral of a Hell's Angels biker I had led to the Lord. All kinds of rough guys from motorcycle gangs were there with their "old ladies." I took advantage of the opportunity to witness to the gospel of Jesus Christ, and I was able to lead eight more to Him.

After the funeral, I went over to the house to spend a few minutes with the friends. They were all drinking and taking dope, but it was an opportunity to witness the gospel to all the people there.

I've married couples from the hip movement who have given their hearts to Jesus during my counseling. They wanted the ceremony to be held outdoors, and they wanted their hip friends there.

So I married them at a nearby park, some at San Pedro Park and some at Griffith Park, in the Los Angeles area. All of their friends would come to the park, but they wouldn't have come to a church. During the explanation of what marriage is all about I was able to explain the way to salvation, how God loves us, how Jesus came, and how we can receive Him as our Lord and Saviour.

I had the joy of seeing people converted at the end of those

wedding ceremonies because I took advantage of the opportunit
and was willing to go out there where the people were to presen
the message of Christ.

Another important place to tell the news about how Christ ca
change lives is in a house of prostitution, where your encounte
might go something like this.

You ring the buzzer and someone peeks out and says, "Wh
are you here?"

Then you say, "I'm here for the right reason. I'd like to see th
girls."

They'll take you in and bring out some girls, and you reach
in your pocket and pull out some Jesus stickers and tracts an
your Bible. Then you say, "Girls, I'm a Christian, and I want t
give you some gospel material. I'm not here to try to embarras
you; I'm here to share with you about how you can have a new
life with Jesus," and you start sharing about Christ.

All they can do is throw you out or kill you. If they throw yo
out, you can pray on your way out the door. If they kill you, yo
go to heaven, so you have nothing to lose and everything to wir

You have to take that attitude if you want to be successful in
winning the various types of social outcasts to Christ. As a com
mitted Christian, you can't just overlook the people who live an
work in the notorious sin spots.

## HOME FELLOWSHIP

This is a vital part of the Jesus revolution. This in my min
should supplement the church, though often it *is* the church fo
many people.

These meetings take place in homes, apartments, even offic
buildings. A small group of Christians meet once a week or se
eral times a week at a certain place. Even in between meeting
they can call one another for prayer requests, etc.

The meetings generally center around prayers, with mos
people present praying aloud, praying for needs, and praisin
God. There then follows Bible study with group discussior
Singing and sharing answered prayers and prayer requests ar
mixed with testimonies. Often the Lord's Supper is shared wit
bread and juice.

Many times this is a meeting that new converts will atten

with you even though they object to going to church. Often, too, many people will be led into church through these meetings. As a result of this fact many churches encourage home Bible fellowship, and count this as a vital part of their outreach. This type of fellowship is truly important for new converts in areas where there is no church fellowship that is really turned on!

## CHURCH

God uses many groups, organizations, and persons for His glory, but it is from the Bible that we see the perfect plan of God to use the church as the base of evangelism, worship, and training. We do not need a new Saviour, a new Bible, or a new Revelation—but we do need a spiritual, alive, repentant, powerful, victorious church!

A new breath of Holy Spirit fire is being received by God's people meeting together in assemblies all around the world. Churches that only a month ago were almost dead and defeated are now alive and overflowing.

Recently in the British Isles we spoke to overflow crowds in huge churches that had not been filled in living memory for gospel services. I do not encourage people to leave the church, I say *stay in*, and *let's have revival*. I was saved in a church parking lot, baptized in a church, learned to preach in a church, preached my first sermon in a church, was ordained in a church, pastored churches, led in starting seven churches, am a member of a church now, and preach in hundreds of churches. I love the church; God is at work in the church. I criticize things in many churches yet I also see great revival. Many churches in the world today are truly going for God.

Let the church reach out! Stones, pews, steeples, and crosses are not holy—they can't save, but Jesus can.—Let's share *Him*.— As we worship let it be in joy and holiness; as we serve let it be in compassion; as we witness let us talk of repentance and dedicated discipleship.

Regular church services can be filled with a new life and power. Bible study groups can lead in strong discipleship. An evangelism committee can lead the church out into every area of community witness. Special rallies and revival meetings can be held combined with outreaches like many of those already

given in this book. Late night Jesus rallies held at midnight or
even later can often reach people coming out of the nightclubs,
movies, etc. The church can be the powerhouse to shake the
community, city, and world. "Let It Be."

## OPPORTUNITIES UNLIMITED

The main thing is to see every place we go and every thing
we do as a wide-open opportunity for ministry. If only we were
conscious of witnessing all the time. Wherever we are, we
should be looking for ways to spread the good news by talking
about Jesus, by using Jesus stickers and tracts, by greeting people
with "God bless you" or "Jesus loves you" instead of just a "hi"
or "hello." There are countless other ways. Here are some ex-
amples of what I mean, showing how a person can have victory
for Christ even under the most unlikely conditions:

●  While I was walking down the street or sitting in an airport terminal, guys have come up to me and said, "Hey, man!
We're having a swinging party—you know, some chicks and dope
and all that. Would you like to come?" When I get an invitation
like that I always accept. I go to the party, and when they start
passing the drugs or the booze I say, "No, I gave my heart to
Jesus, and I don't need to do that. I'm filled with the Spirit."

Then they'll say, unbelievingly, *"What?"* and the whole party
grinds to a halt.

At that point I pull out my Bible and start witnessing. "Sure,
man," I tell them, "I like to go to a party because it's a great
opportunity to talk about Jesus." I don't start really condemning
them, but just start sharing about what Jesus does, and their
minds are blown.

●  If I'm going down the street and some guy says, "Would
you like to meet a girl down here?" I say, "Yes, sure."

Then I go down with him, and when he introduces me to the
girl I ask, "Are you saved?" That will usually make them ask
something like, "What are you?" and I say, "I'm a preacher.
This guy asked me if I wanted to meet a girl and I said I did,
because I want everybody to be saved."

●  If I'm sitting in a bar and someone is playing the piano,
sometimes he'll ask, "Does anyone have a request?" I always call
out "Amazing Grace" or some other gospel song.

●  If I'm around a person who says a curse word, I just

iile pleasantly and say, "Do you know Him?" The person will ually ask, "Know who?" and then I say, "The One you were lking about. You know, He's my Lord. He really changed my e."

So even when a person curses it can give you an opportunity begin making an inroad to witness. I've found that you can ways get your shot in somewhere for Jesus if that's what you're oking for.

### Violence

Now, let me say something about violence, or the risk of tting assaulted during a Jesus march or when you're picket-g, or maybe when you're out witnessing to a rough group.

Of course, you should try never to antagonize anyone. Never to force anything on anybody that he doesn't want. And you ould do everything you can to try to prevent being attacked. it in spite of all that, say you are attacked. What do you do?

First of all, your Bible may be able to help you ward off vio- ace. You should always have your Bible with you when you e out witnessing, and you can keep it between you and your tacker. Then he'll have to strike the Bible before he can strike u, and this is often a deterrent. Many people just hate to ock the Bible out of the way.

Do not fear. Remember that Jesus is with you. So get calmly wn on your knees and place your face down between your gs with your shoulders up so that your arms cover your ears d the sides of your head. This is a protective position of ayer, but most people won't realize that at the same time you elt in prayer you also covered the parts of your body that are ost sensitive to being hit.

As the person attacks you, pray. Usually, it's best to pray out ud, calling for God to deal with him. Pray for the person, and him know that you love him.

If another person is being attacked, you need to throw your- lf between him and the antagonist. Just get in between them, d then they have to attack you. If there are several in your oup, when you start getting beaten up someone else will step and take the attack, and that way you just keep on throwing fresh bodies, each one protecting the others.

Sometimes the problem might be obscene gestures, or guys

trying to pick up girls in the group or to play with their bodi
Many times the girls can handle things very well if they j
keep their Bibles out front and make the guys keep their han
off them. If someone tries to grab a girl, she can say, "Here,
you want to hold something, hold the Bible."

If profanity is going to cause you to fight, you had better n
plan to go out. Instead of reacting violently to cursing, eve:
body should just smile and say, "Jesus loves you," and keep
with what they're doing.

To see how the Lord can reach out and change the life of
violent, profane person is a wonderful thing. It is one of t
richest rewards of bringing people to Christ. I've seen it happe
hundreds of times. Here is a striking example of it:

One night outside our place on Sunset Strip a big fell
named James was beating two girls; they were in awful shape
stepped between them and they ran into our building. I
threatened to kill me, and ordered me to move. When I did
he picked up a bottle, broke it and put it at my throat. I sa
"You can kill me, but I love you and so does Jesus." I knelt a
began to pray for him. He started kicking me, then finally
stopped and after a bit I looked up. He was sitting on the ste
crying. He said, "Arthur, I've never known such love, help me
Now he walks the Sunset Strip, Bible in hand leading others
Jesus!

# After the Witnessing

**FOLLOW-UP**

A most vital part of telling the word of Jesus is to provide the best help possible for new converts. This depends a great deal on where you lead the person to Jesus.

If the person converted lives near you and has an immediate interest in church then the follow-up is fairly simple if your church has a new-convert training class. If the person does not want to attend your church, then the teaching should be done by you in the house or in a house fellowship.

Oftentimes in high school or college there are Christian organizations that one can get involved in that provide excellent training. You can meet with a friend you led to Jesus during lunch hours, or before or after work. In essence follow-up can be done anytime, anywhere.

Remember, a new convert may not automatically love the church. (His knowledge of the church or the one he once attended may have turned him off.) Also, he may not accept all your standards of life. Fear not! Teach that person the Bible, and the Holy Spirit will lead them to the truth. Here is an example of this:

One night in a nightclub in Las Vegas, Nevada I led one of the leading strippers to Jesus between her dancing acts. She truly gave her heart to Jesus in repentance and faith, however she just didn't have the strength to quit her job, her only source of money. It was my last night preaching in the city and I had to leave. The pastor of the church I was preaching in, the Reverend Jim Reed, went right into the club to teach the lady the Bible. A Bible study in the dressing room of a huge gambling casino show room! Yes! Four days later she quit, was baptized, remarried her husband and now has a wonderful house for God!

That follow-up changed her. What if the pastor had refused to go? He is now the minister of the Las Vegas strip!

Another example is a young man who was converted in His Place after he wandered in and out of church. He was taking pills and was bitter at the church. A runaway from a minister's home, he wanted nothing to do with church people, yet he studied the Bible in our Jesus house, began going to church with the people, joined our team, and is now a strong Christian disciple, loving and serving in the church he once hated.

Sometimes the follow-up is brief. When you lead someone to Jesus who lives in another city and is just passing through, you need to get his name, address, and phone number so you can contact someone there to visit him. Also give the new convert the name of an "on fire" Christian or church to contact. If you are running an outreach ministry you should provide information on new converts to ministers who will do the follow-up for you.

It is good if possible for you to write a personal note to the person you led to Jesus, even if they live far away. You can also enroll each person you win to Jesus in good new-convert correspondence courses.

The key to follow-up I believe is the immediate contact following the salvation of the person. Sometimes you have no way to contact the person again. No matter what. . . .

A.  Make sure the person is sure of his salvation. Show him Scripture passages of assurance (2 Corinthians 5:18, 1 John 1:9; 5:13, Romans 10:9, 10, 13, Revelation 3:20, John 3:16, 36).

B.  Pray daily. Live in a spirit of prayer and let Jesus be your closest friend. You'll never get stronger than the amount of time you spend in prayer (1 Thessalonians 5:17, Luke 18:1).

C.  Read the Bible daily. Jesus said, " . . . Man shall not live by bread alone, but by every word that proceedeth out of the mouth of God" (Matthew 4:4). Also refer to Acts 17:11 and Psalms 1:2.

D.  Witness for Christ daily. I like to teach the new convert how to lead a person to Jesus and then, before I leave him I find a person for him to share the fact that he has received Jesus as his Lord. In other words I feel a new convert needs to immediately begin witnessing. Then he will never have a fear of sharing Christ; it is just natural.

E. Confess Christ openly and be baptized. (Baptism does not forgive sin, but is a symbol of a new birth and an act of obedience to Christ.) A person should not be ashamed to openly confess Jesus as Lord. Then we encourage that person to be baptized as soon as possible, the same day or night if possible. This is the policy of the New Testament Christian. A church baptism, or one in a lake, ocean, swimming pool, or river is fine (Matthew 10:32; 28:19, 20; Acts 2:41).

F. Attend church where the Bible is preached and Christ is honored. To become part of a local fellowship of Christians is very vital to Christian growth.

G. Keep Christ's commandments as Jesus said, "If ye love me, keep my commandments (John 14:15).

This is only a beginning but it lays the groundwork for future growth. I like to give the person some gospel tracts and a New Testament with the notation:

> *Your new birth date is:* (date)
> *Signed:* (signature of new convert)

## Personal Witnessing

### TELLING A PERSON OF SALVATION

I believe we should witness for Christ everywhere we go. I normally use a direct question although often I may vary the approach depending on where I am.

I might begin with the question, Should you die right now, do you have the assurance you would go to heaven? Should the answer be no, then I share. I say that I'm sure they would not

mind me showing them some Scriptures. I then read Roman
6:23: "For the wages of sin is death; but the gift of God is eternal
life through Jesus Christ our Lord."

I say Satan tempts us to sin and all have sinned (Romans 3:23).
For sin we get something—wages—the wages of sin is death. This
means separation from God eternally, but God has preached a
gift. A gift is free, however it must be received. This gift is
eternal life and we receive this gift through Jesus Christ when
we allow Him to be Lord of our life.

We are separated from God by sin. How can we cross over
this gulf of sin? Through repentance of sin and faith in Jesus, we
cross over and in that moment we are saved. Share 1 John 1:7,9
Revelation 3:2; John 3:16, 2 Corinthians 5:17. Which side are
you on right now? I'm sure you would like to repent and have
Jesus in your heart.

You can pray right now and give your heart to him. Lets pray
You can pray this prayer right now:

> Dear God, I need you. I open my heart and repent of
> my sins. Jesus I believe you died for my sins and rose
> again. Come into my heart and save my soul. Take con-
> trol of my life and fill me with your Holy Spirit. Thank
> you for hearing my prayer, in Jesus' name I pray.
> Amen.

I then give the follow-up.

My final challenge is that through the power of the Holy
Spirit it is essential for each of us to take advantage of every
contact, every opportunity, every possible means of proclaiming
the gospel of Jesus Christ. Let's **TELL THE WORLD!**

---

For More Information or Materials Write:

**Arthur Blessitt**
**Evangelistic Association**
**PO Box 46216**
**Hollywood, Calif. 90046**